USE WITH
**2ND EDITION**

TECHNIQUE & ARTISTRY BOOK

with Scales

LEVEL 4

# PIANO
*Adventures*® *by Nancy and Randall Faber*
THE BASIC PIANO METHOD

## CONTENTS

**FABER**
PIANO ADVENTURES®
3042 Creek Drive
Ann Arbor, Michigan 48108

2/8/24

# LEVEL 4 TECHNIQUE SECRETS

These four Technique Secrets are used as daily warm-ups for the exercises and pieces in this book.
The "secrets" may be learned gradually and are highlighted in gold boxes throughout the pages.

**The teacher should demonstrate each "technique secret" as it is introduced.**

1. **The first secret is** ALIGNMENT

    Alignment refers to the balance of arm weight in a straight line
    through your forearm, hand, and to the knuckle over the fingertip.

    • After the grace notes, balance your arm weight
      over each half note.

    • Hold and check for a "tall knuckle."

    **Balance Beam**

2. **The second secret is** DROP and FOLLOW-THROUGH

    • Drop with arm weight to release a "spark" of energy that
      carries your fingers through the pattern.

    **Spark the Pattern**

Continue the L.H. pattern on
E, F, G, A, B, and C.

Continue the R.H. pattern on
C, B, A, G, F, and E.

**3.** **The third secret is** WEIGHTED TONE (and EMPTY FINGERS)

To produce different "tonal colors," change the amount of arm weight.
How smoothly can you make the tonal colors change through this passage?

- Begin with "empty fingers"—*unweighted* touch (*pp*).

- Gradually change to a *weighted* tone by transferring
  arm weight from finger to finger.

**Tonal Colors**

**Listening for color**

**Listening for color**

**4.** **The fourth secret is** HALF CIRCLE / FULL CIRCLE

Wrist circles help transfer arm weight for proper alignment on each finger.
Half-circles can be used for smooth, wide leaps, such as this L.H. accompaniment.

- Release finger 5 as you pivot on finger 2.

- Your wrist should rise gracefully to play a *light* thumb.

**Lead with the Wrist**

**Gracefully and slowly**

Lesson p.10 (Maple Leaf Rag), p.12 (Hall of the Mountain King)

2/12/24

Warm-up with *Balance Beam* (p. 2).

- What do you notice about the fingering in contrary motion?
- Learn and play by memory.

# C Scale in Contrary Motion
**Two Octaves**

**Listening carefully**

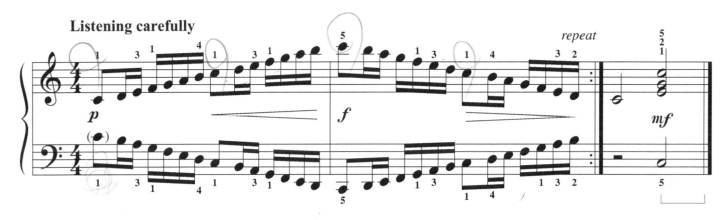

# Scale Toccata in C
from Op. 101

- First practice hands alone.
- Then learn hands together and play by memory.

Ferdinand Beyer
(1803-1863, Germany)
original form

**Steadily**

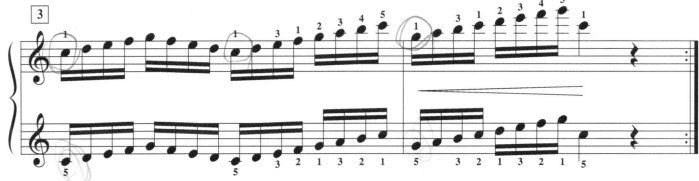

____ ♪ = 72 *Andante*     ____ ♪ = 104 *Moderato*     ____ ♪ = 132 *Allegro*     ____ ♩ = 72

2/22/24

Technique Secret:

## alignment

Warm-up with *Balance Beam* (p. 2).

- As you move from finger 5 to finger 3, balance your arm weight in a straight line through your forearm, hand, and to the knuckle over the fingertip.

- Learn and play by memory.

**Hold the damper pedal down throughout for each exercise.**

# Make a Mountain

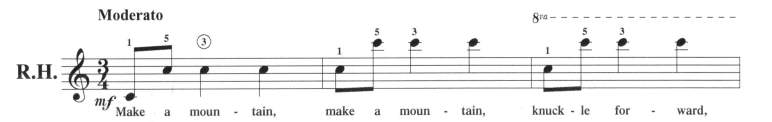

R.H. Moderato
Make a moun - tain, make a moun - tain, knuck - le for - ward,
make a moun - tain, make a moun - tain, knuck - le for - ward.

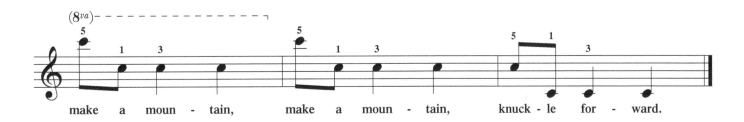

L.H. Moderato
Make a moun - tain, make a moun - tain, knuck - le for - ward,

make a moun - tain, make a moun - tain, knuck - le for - ward.

FF3012

📖 Lesson p.8 (Two-Octave Scales)

## drop and follow-through

Warm-up with *Spark the Pattern* (p. 2).

- Drop into each L.H. accented note. The R.H. 8th notes "follow through" to complete the broken chord pattern.

- Memorize this etude.

# Maple Leaf Etude

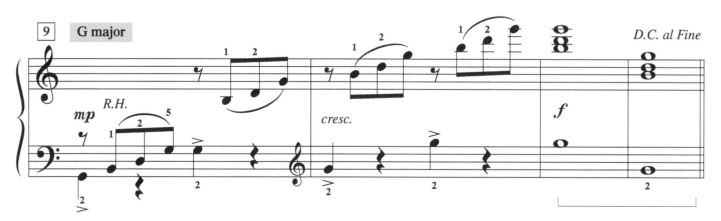

_____ ♩ = 80 *Andante*      _____ ♩ = 96 *Moderato*      _____ ♩ = 116-132 *Allegro*

## weighted tone / empty fingers

Warm-up with *Tonal Colors* (p. 3).

• Practice the R.H. alone for fingering and forearm alignment.

• Then practice H.T. (hands together).
At *measures 3-4*, use a weighted tone on the accents and use "empty fingers" on the *staccatos*.

# Windy Scales

**Key of _____ Major**

Carl Czerny
(1791-1857, Austria)
original form

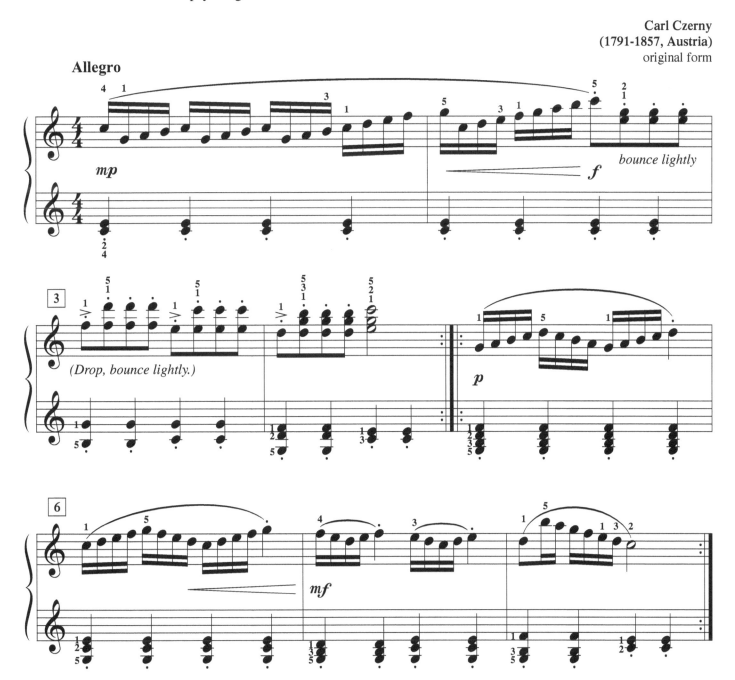

_____ ♩ = 60 *Andante*       _____ ♩ = 80 *Moderato*       _____ ♩ = 96 *Allegro*

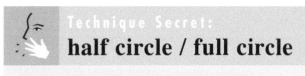

# The Mountain King
## 1. In the Great Hall

This broken chord pattern moves from **A minor** to **C major**. The arrows indicate the circular wrist motion.

• Play by memory.

• When you are comfortable with *legato* circles, play the R.H. *staccato*.
  Use the same wrist circles as used for *legato*.

## 2. Chased by the Trolls

Lesson p.12 (Hall of the Mountain King)

FF3012

**Full Circle Warm-up**

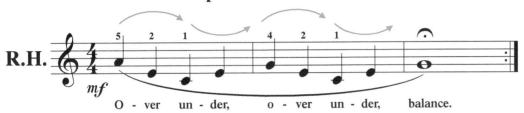

R.H.

*mf*

O - ver un - der,   o - ver un - der,   balance.

- Make a small wrist circle for each group of four 16th notes. The warm-up above prepares the circular motion.

- Play by memory.

## 3. Successful Escape

**Quick march**

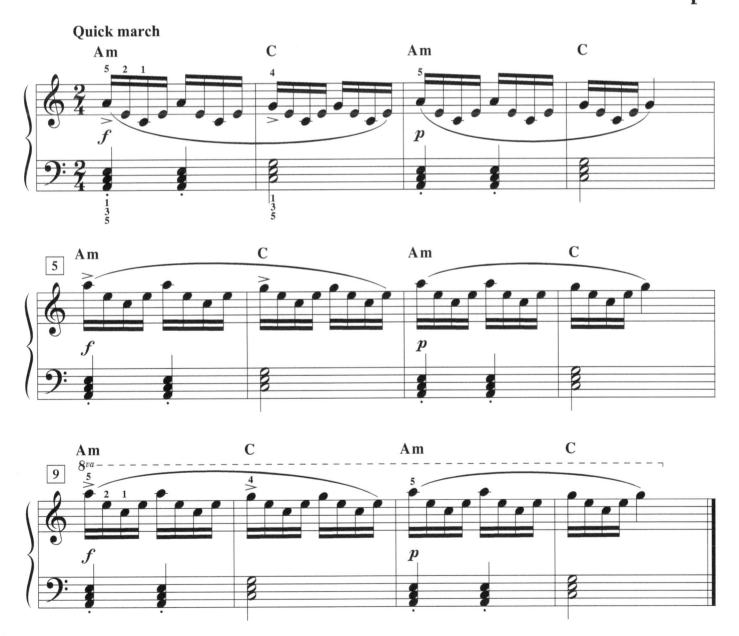

This Artistry Magic piece will help you practice shaping phrases that use a TWO-HAND GESTURE.

- For each **motive** (short musical idea), the L.H. drops and the R.H. follows through to complete the pattern.

- Hint: Be sure to follow all the <  and  > marks as you play.

## Excalibur*

**Key of** ____ **Major/minor** (circle)

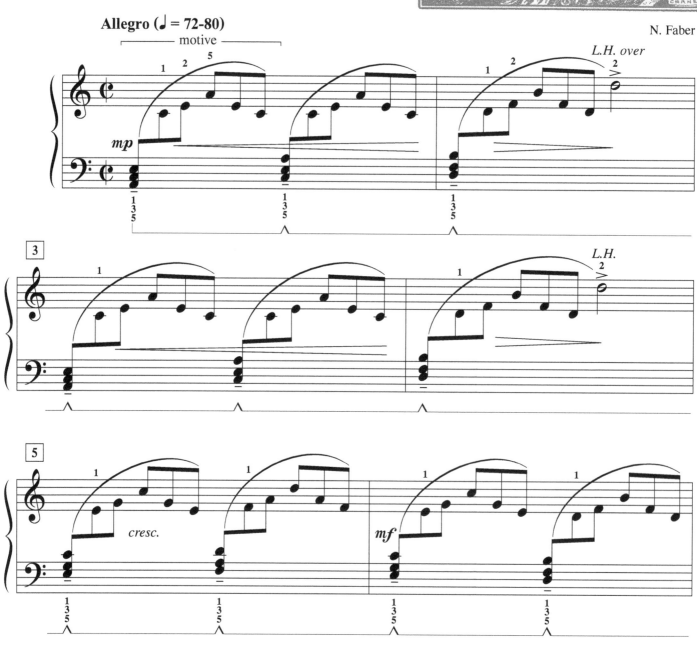

*Excalibur was the magical sword of the legendary King Arthur.

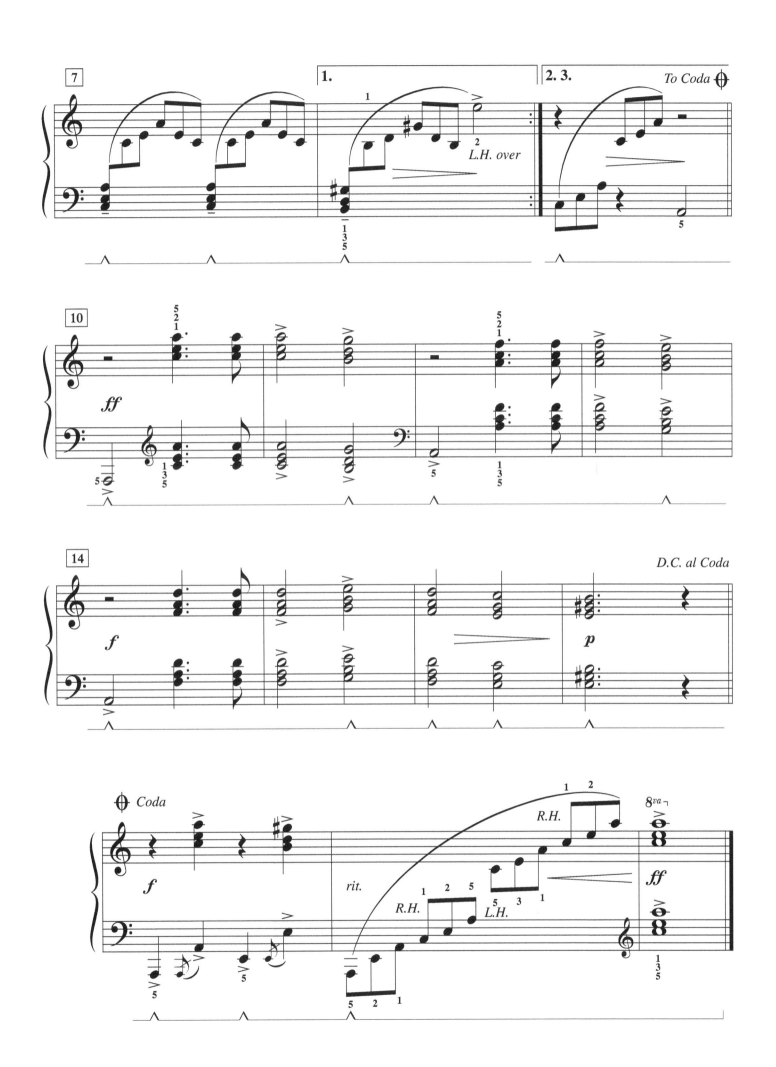

# Dueling High School Bands

## 1. The Wampus Cats

**Technique Secret:**
**drop and follow-through**

Warm-up with *Spark the Pattern* (p. 2).

- Drop on each accent to "spark" the triplet pattern.
- Play by memory.

**Allegro moderato**

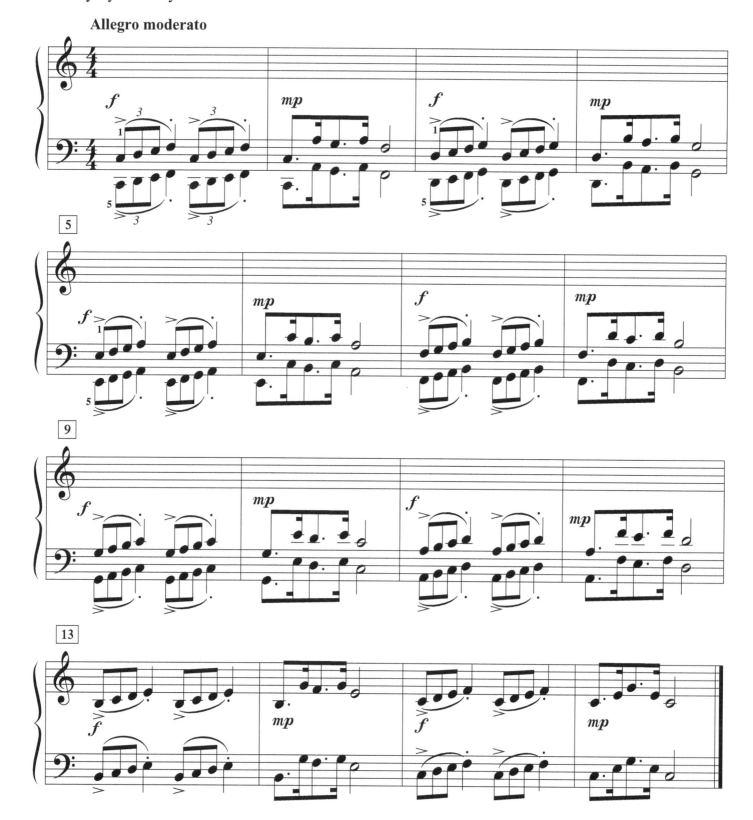

Lesson p.16 (Dotted-Eighth to Sixteenth Pattern)

FF3012

- Similar to *The Wampus Cats*, use the accented note to spark each pattern.

- Play by memory.

## 2. The Thunder Hawks

This theme is from one of Beethoven's most famous sonatas. The tempo is marked *Adagio* (pronounced ah-DAH-jyoh), meaning slowly.

- Would you play the opening R.H. triplets with a weighted touch or "empty fingers"?

- The melody enters at *measure 5*. Bring it to the forefront with a weighted touch, in contrast to the "empty fingers" of the triplets.

- Where does the R.H. go back to "empty fingers?"

## Moonlight Sonata

**Key of _____ Major/minor**

Ludwig van Beethoven
(1770-1827, Germany)
arranged

Lesson p.18 (Allegro Grazioso)

FF3012

Technique Secret:
## drop and follow-through

Warm-up with *Spark the Pattern* (p. 2).

CHORDS

• Memorize this L.H. chord inversion workout.

# Virtuoso Chord Patterns
### (for L.H. alone)

____ ♩. = 60 *Andante*   ____ ♩. = 80 *Moderato*   ____ ♩. = 100 *Allegretto*

**Technique Secret:**
## alignment

Warm-up with *Balance Beam* (p. 2).

- Use the accent at the beginning of each measure to "spark" the pattern.

- Memorize this R.H. scale workout.

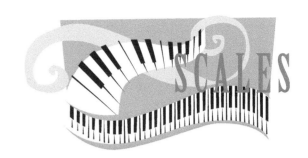

# Virtuoso Scale Patterns
### (for R.H. alone)

**F Major**

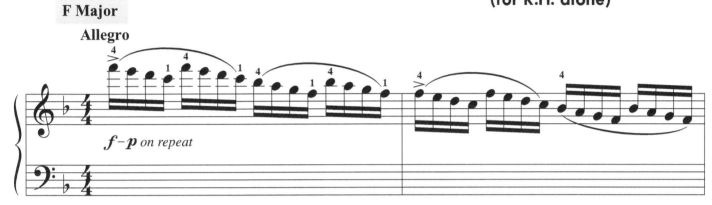

**D minor**

____ ♩ = 60 *Andante*   ____ ♩ = 80 *Moderato*   ____ ♩ = 104-112 *Allegro*

*Silver Rain Etude* has many TONAL COLORS, from the opening *piano* to the final *forte*.

- First learn the notes and fingering. Finding patterns will help you.
  Can you find a broken chord pattern for the **A7** chord?

- Vary your weighted touch to match the dynamic marks.

- Review: For *measures 8-9*, use **rotation**, a back and forth rocking motion of the hand.
  (Rotation is a Technique Secret taught in Level 3A.)

# Silver Rain Etude

**Key of \_\_\_\_ Major/minor**

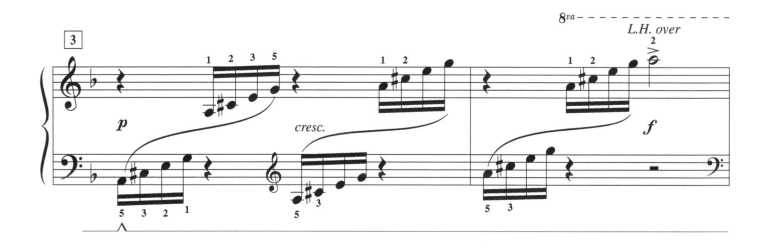

Lesson p.27 (French Minuet)                                     FF3012

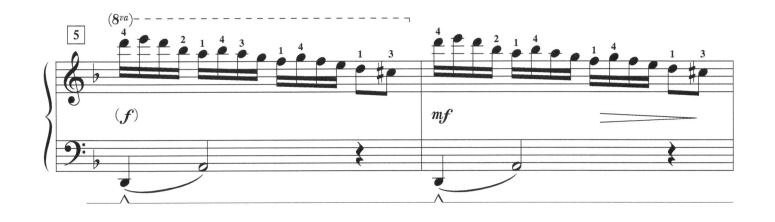

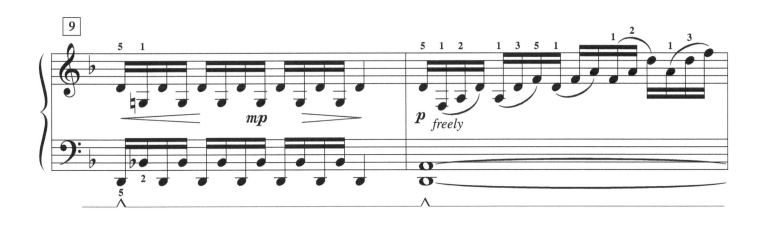

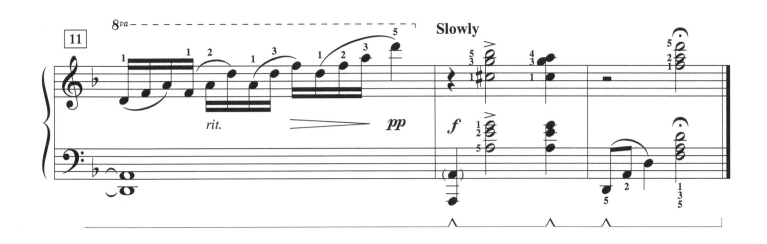

**Technique Secret:**

## alignment

Warm-up with *Balance Beam* (p. 2).

# G Scale in Contrary Motion

### Two Octaves

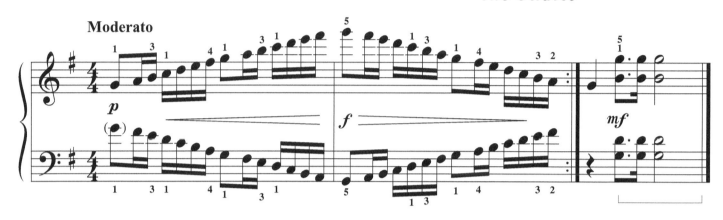

# Scale Toccata in G

Op. 101, No. 91

Carl Czerny
(1791-1857, Austria)
original form

_____ ♪ = 72 *Andante*      _____ ♪ = 104 *Moderato*      _____ ♪ = 132 *Allegro*      _____ ♩ = 72

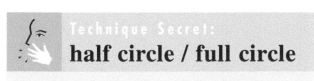

**Technique Secret:**
## half circle / full circle

Warm-up with *Lead with the Wrist* (p. 3).

The words describe the circular wrist motion.

# Circle Shapes

Key of ____ Major/minor

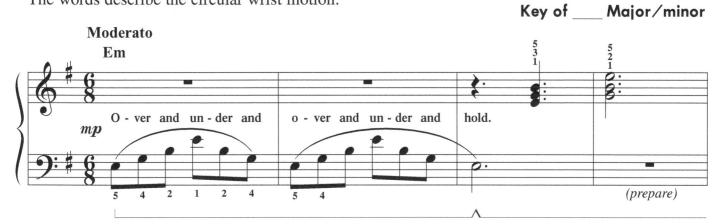

Lesson p.32 (Volga Boatmen)

## weighted tone / empty fingers

Warm-up with *Tonal Colors* (p. 3).

- Play each 16th note quickly and lightly into the 8th note that follows.

- Use "empty fingers" (unweighted touch) for the *piano*, *leggiero* tone.

- Use a weighted touch for the *forte* passages.

# Chasing Butterflies
Op. 63, No. 11

### Key of _____ Major/minor

Jean Louis Streabbog
(1835-1886, Belgium)
original form

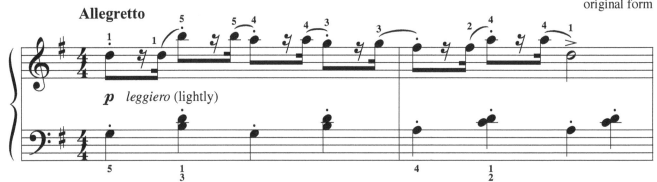

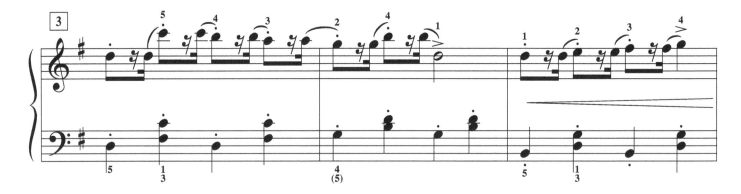

Technique Secret:
## weighted tone / empty fingers

Warm-up with *Tonal Colors* (p. 3).

- Listen for "two voices" by holding the thumb while the other voice is played.

# Inner Voices

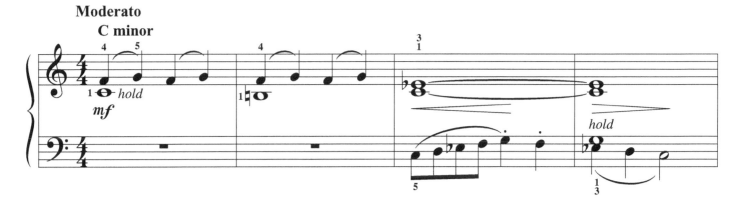

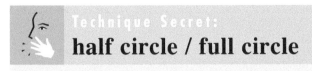

**Technique Secret:**

## half circle / full circle

Warm-up with *Lead with the Wrist* (p. 3).

### L.H. Accompaniment Hints
- Pivot on finger 2 for a smooth, relaxed gesture.
- Play the thumb *lightly* with a rising wrist.

# Brushstrokes
### (for L.H. alone)

**Expressively**

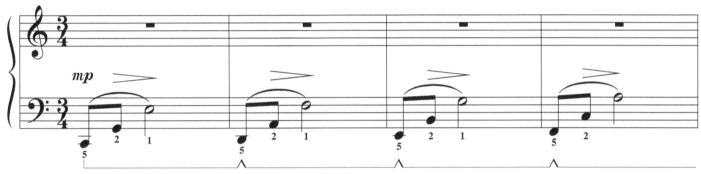

Key change:
___ Major

‿⌃ *pedal simile (pedal similarly)*

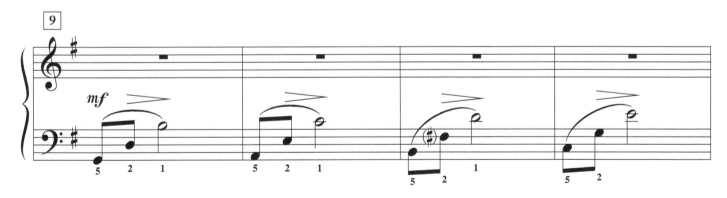

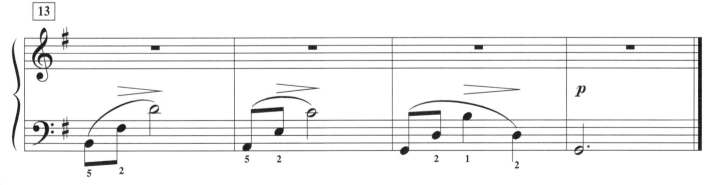

◁▷ Lesson p.35 (Chanson)

Artistry at the piano requires effective technical gestures to create contrasting tonal colors, such as BALANCE BETWEEN THE HANDS.

- **R.H. melody:** Think of your R.H. as a singer. Use a weighted touch for rich tone and expressive phrase shaping.

- **L.H. accompaniment:** Think of your L.H. as a gentle rolling tide. Keep it subdued. Remember to pivot on finger 2, letting your wrist rise to play a *light* thumb.

# Caspian Sea

Key of ____ Major/minor

**Andante espressivo**

N. Faber

*pedal simile (similarly)*

Lesson p.35 (Chanson)

**Chord Check:** Can you write the chord names in the boxes from *measure 9* to the end?

# Playing in Sharp Keys

 **Technique Secret:**
### alignment

Warm-up with *Balance Beam* (p. 2).

## D Scale in Octaves

**Listening carefully**

## Primary Chords in D Major

**Technique Secret:**
### half circle / full circle

Warm-up with *Lead with the Wrist* (p. 3).

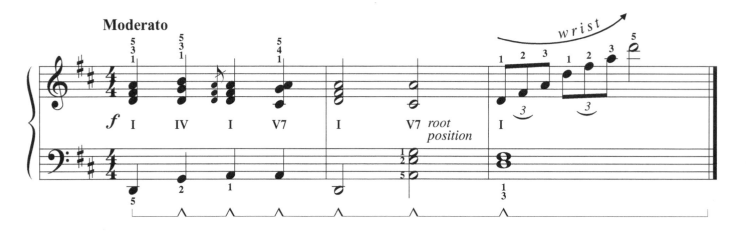

Lesson p.39 (Two-Octave Scales in D, A, and E) 

FF3012

## Mini-Etude and Primary Chords in A Major

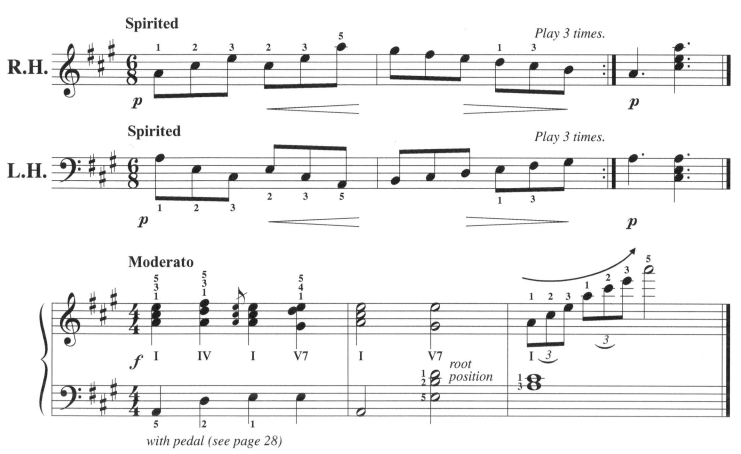

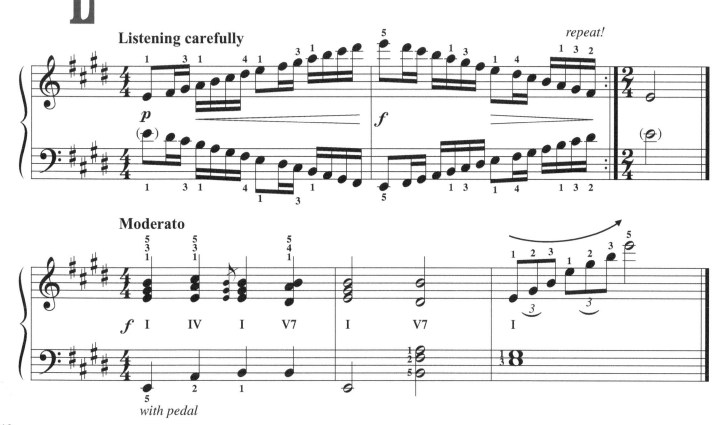

## E Scale in Contrary Motion and Primary Chords

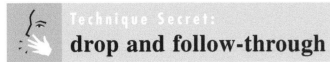

# Return of the Scale Monster!

### Op. 599, No. 69

- First practice slowly. Listen for even, steady scales.

Carl Czerny
(1791-1857, Austria)
original form*

**Allegretto**

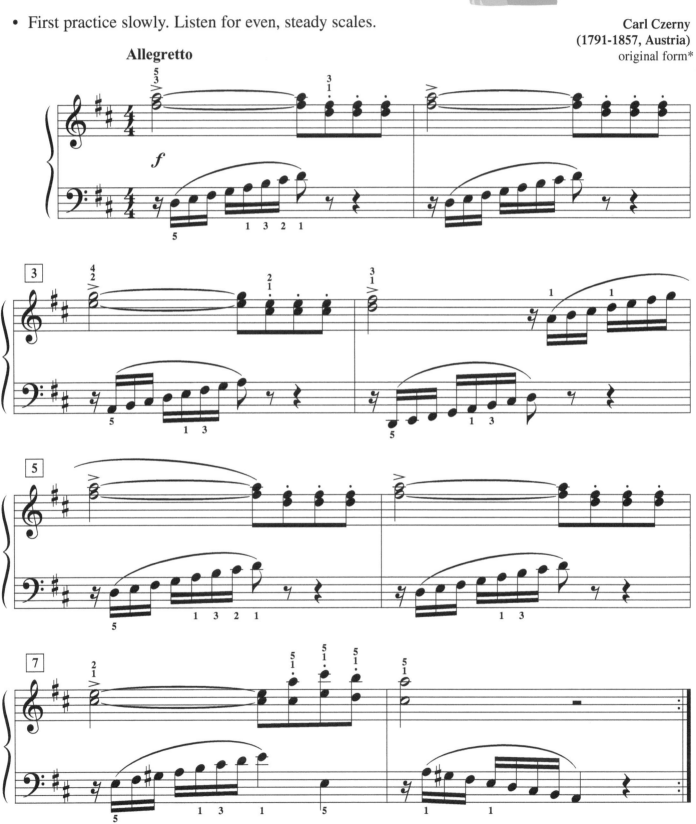

*Originally in 2/4 time.

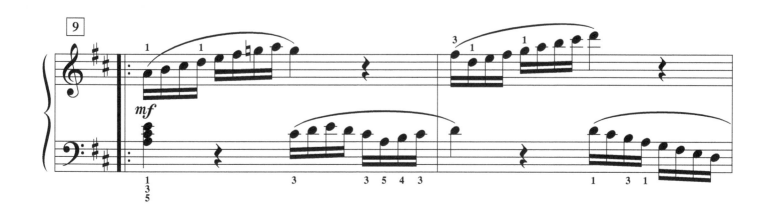

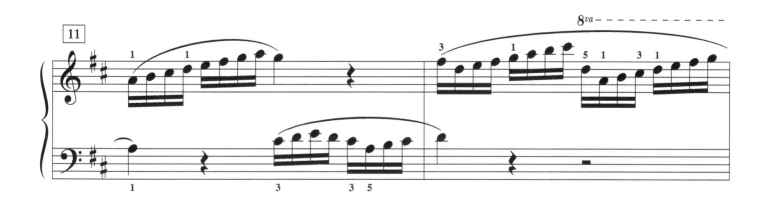

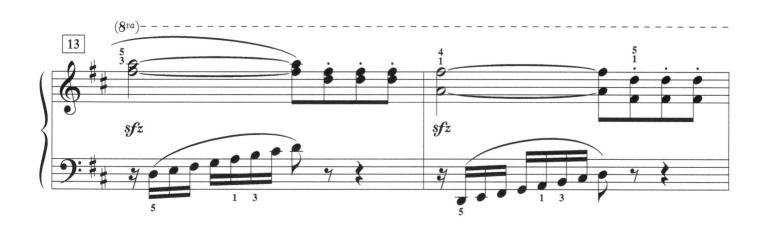

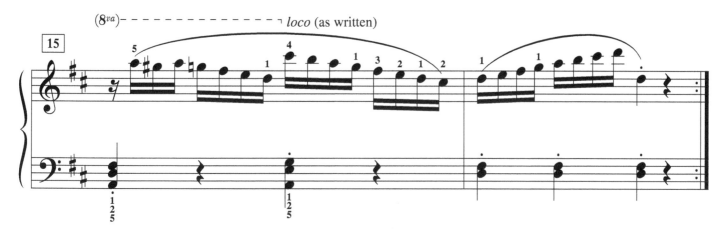

_____ ♩ = 56 *Andante*     _____ ♩ = 72 *Moderato*     _____ ♩ = 96 *Allegretto*

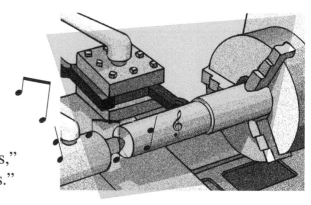

## Technique Secret:
## drop and follow-through

Warm-up with *Spark the Pattern* (p. 2).

- In contrast to a "closed, cupped hand for scale passages," this octave study requires an "open hand for extensions." (See Level 3B Technique Secrets.)

- Drop into each accented L.H. note. The unaccented notes should *lightly* rebound.

# Octave Machine 1

### Key of ____ Major

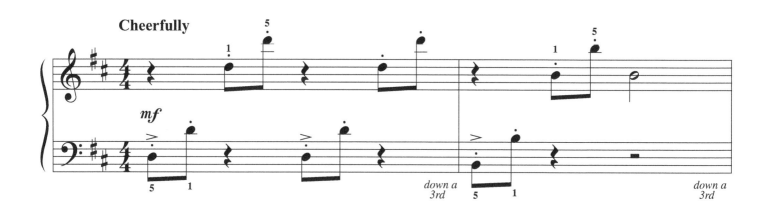

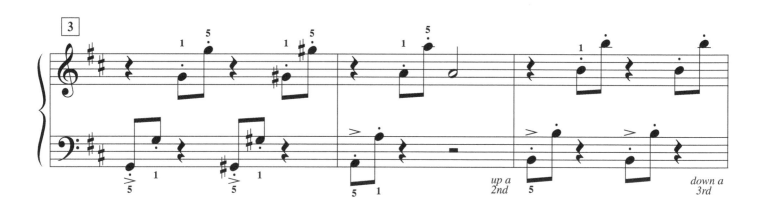

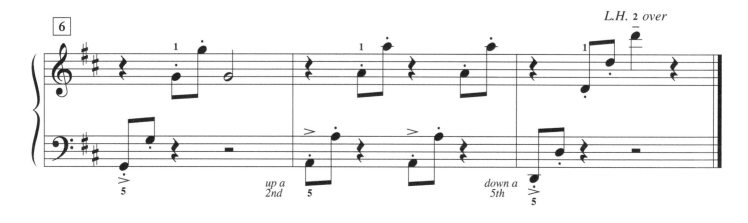

Lesson p.42 (Summer Solstice)

FF3012

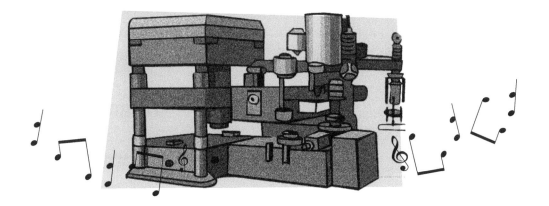

# Octave Machine 2

**Key of \_\_\_\_ Major**

• Think "drop and rebound."

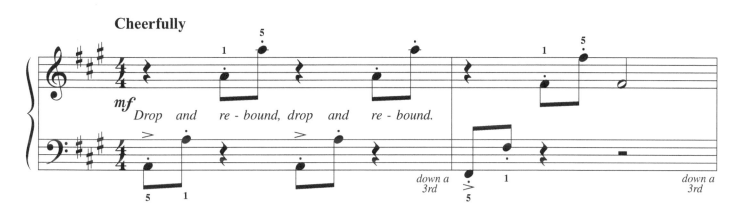

**Cheerfully**

*mf*
Drop and re - bound, drop and re - bound.

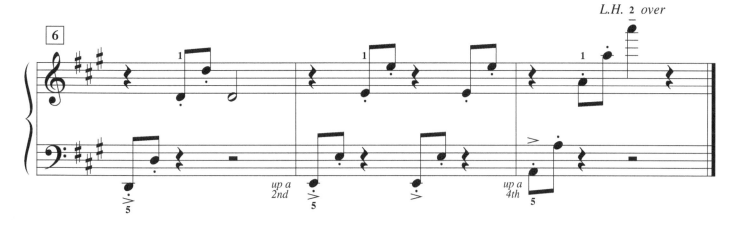

# Right-Hand Finger Races

Hint: Use **rotation*** for *measure 3* of each exercise.

- Practice at slow, medium, and fast tempi.
- Play these exercises by memory.

**Gregarious G Major**

**Dazzling D Major**

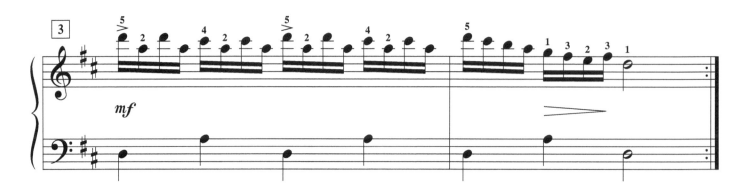

*See page 18 and Level 3A Technique Secret #3.

## Awesome A Major

Lesson p.46 (Wild Flowers)

# Left-Hand Finger Races

Hint: The circled notes will guide you in this 16th-note scale pattern.

- Practice at slow, medium, and fast tempi.
- Play these exercises by memory.

**Grand G Major**

**Daring D Major**

Lesson p.50 (Great Barrier Reef)

FF3012

# Amazing A Major

# Excellent E Major

## Technique & Artistry Check

1. Are you using a half-circle wrist motion to phrase off the R.H.?

2. Are you varying the weighted touch to shape the $<$ and $>$ at measures 11-12?

3. Are you using "drop and follow-through" for the *forte* motives at measure 16?

4. Are you using "empty fingers" for the Coda?

5. Is there a gentle flow to your rhythm, like a midsummer night's breeze?

# A Midsummer Night's Dream

Op. 63, No. 7

### Key of ____ Major/minor

Jean Louis Streabbog
(1835-1886, Belgium)
original form

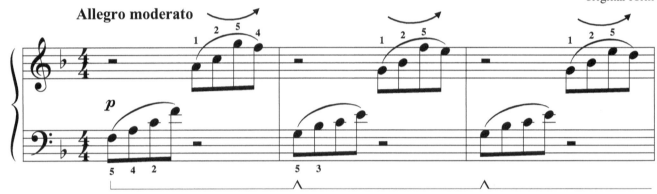

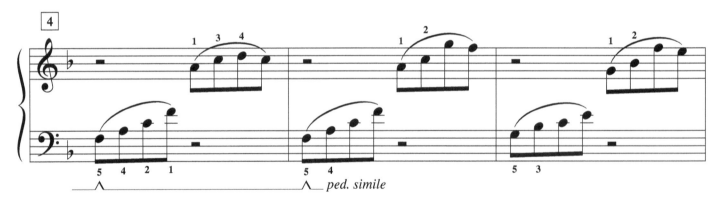

📖 Lesson p.52 (Prelude in C)

FF3012

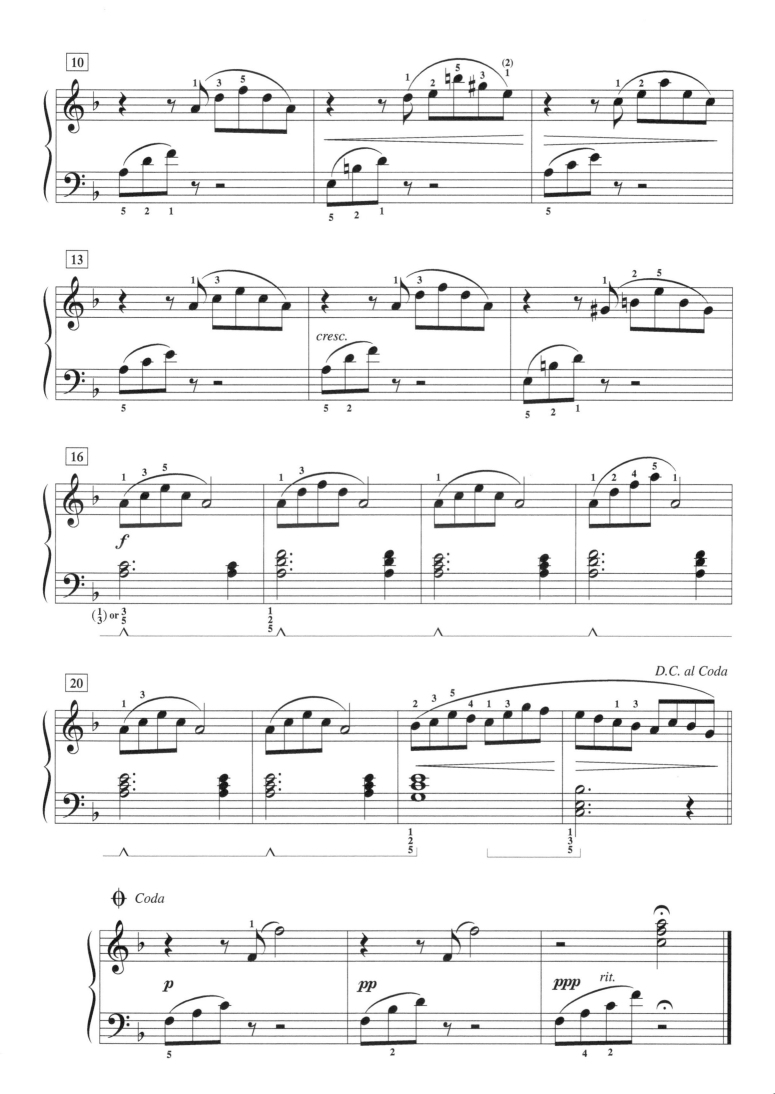

# Two-Octave Major Scales in Parallel Motion

Teachers and students may choose the dynamics for each scale.

- Play hands separately or together.

### C Major

### G Major

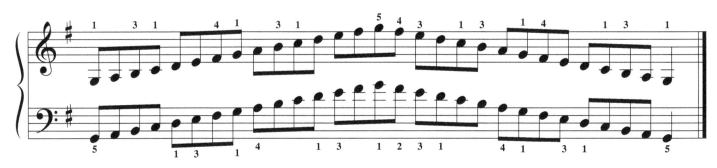

### D Major

### A Major

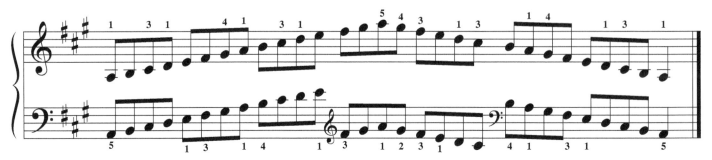

40

**E Major**

**B Major**

**F Major**

**B♭ Major***

**E♭ Major***

*Some students find it useful to learn B♭ and E♭ early for jazz band, festivals, or achievement testing.
These keys are formally introduced in Level 5.

# Two-Octave Major Scales in Contrary Motion

**C Major**

**G Major**

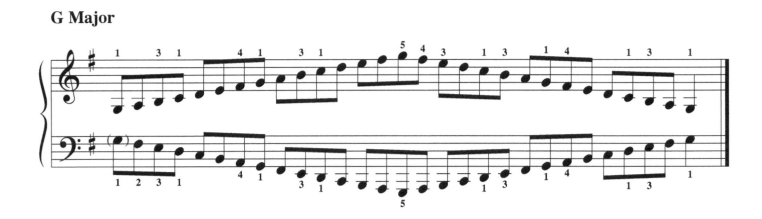

**D Major**

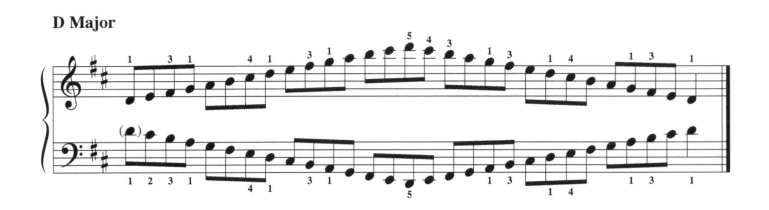

**A Major**

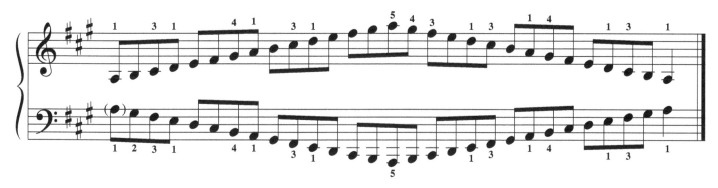

**E Major**

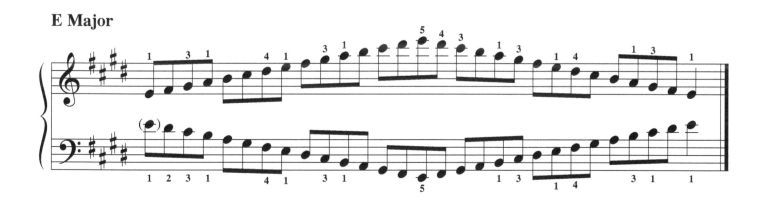

**E♭ Major** (optional)

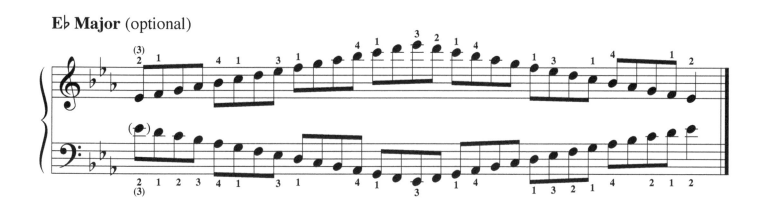

# Two-Octave Minor Scales in Parallel Motion

- Play hands separately or together.

### A harmonic minor*

### A melodic minor

### D harmonic minor

### D melodic minor

*The natural minor scale may be reviewed, if desired (no accidental on scale step 7).

44

## E harmonic minor

## E melodic minor

## B harmonic minor

## B melodic minor

**G harmonic minor**

**G melodic minor**

**C harmonic minor**

**C melodic minor**

# Chromatic Scales

- Memorize this chromatic scale etude that begins on E, then, D, then C.

## For Right Hand

## For Left Hand

# Triads

**C Major (for Right Hand)**

**C Major (for Left Hand)**

**A minor (for Right Hand)**

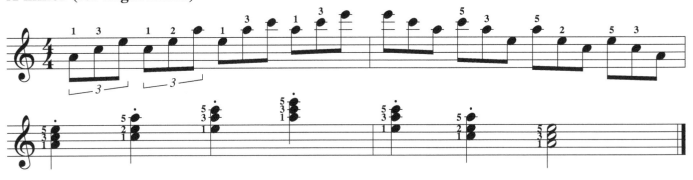

**A minor (for Left Hand)**

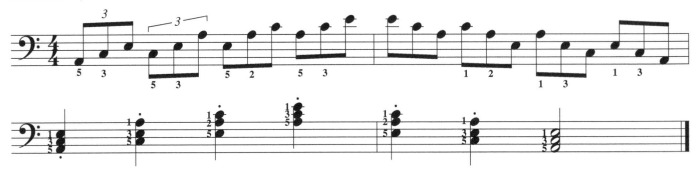

## G Major (for Right Hand)

## G Major (for Left Hand)

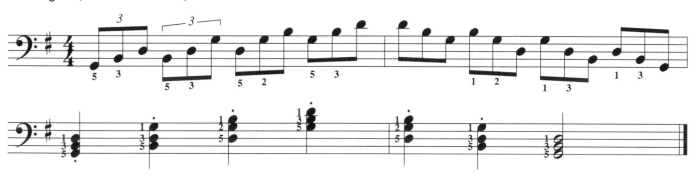

## E minor (for Right Hand)

## E minor (for Left Hand)

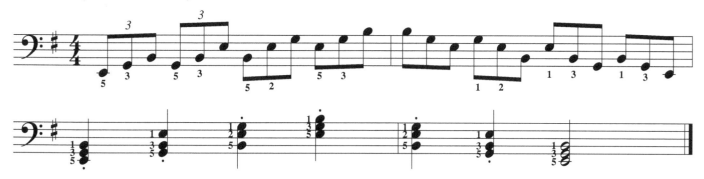

**F Major (for Right Hand)**

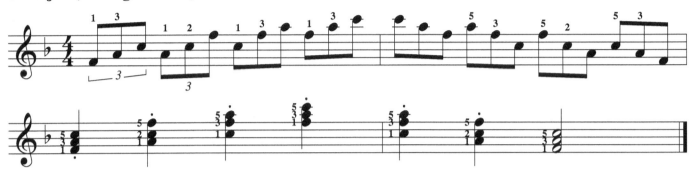

**F Major (for Left Hand)**

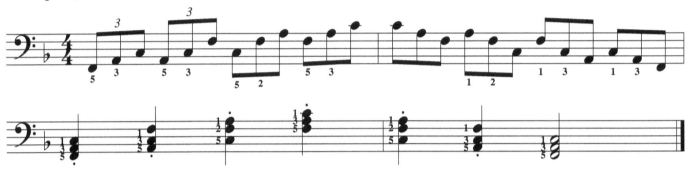

**D minor (for Right Hand)**

**D minor (for Left Hand)**

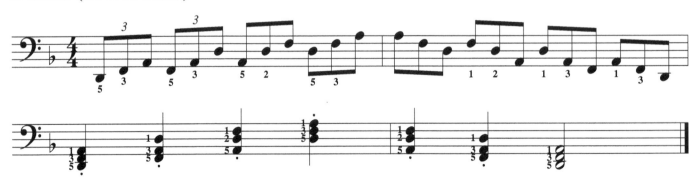

**D Major (for Right Hand)**

**D Major (for Left Hand)**

**B minor (for Right Hand)**

**B minor (for Left Hand)**

**B♭ Major (for Right Hand)**

**B♭ Major (for Left Hand)**

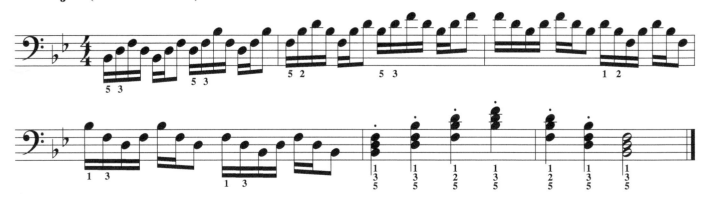

**G minor (for Right Hand)**

**G minor (for Left Hand)**

• Optional: Transpose to **E♭ major** and **C minor**.

FF3012

# Broken Chord Patterns

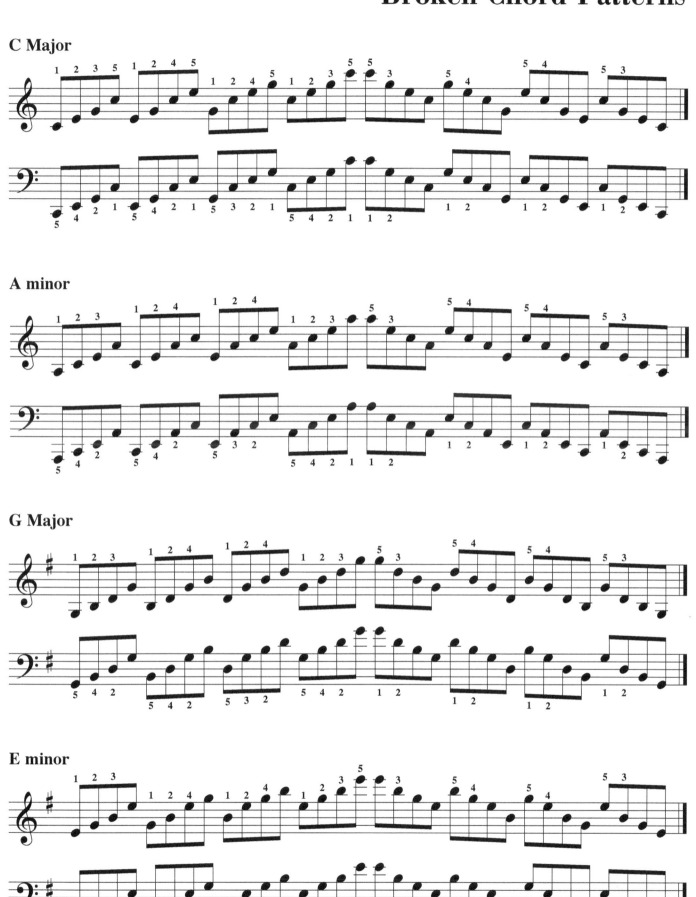

**C Major**

**A minor**

**G Major**

**E minor**

- Optional: Transpose to **F major** and **D minor**.

# Two-Octave Major Arpeggios

The arrows indicate the under and over circular wrist motion for playing arpeggios.

**C Major**

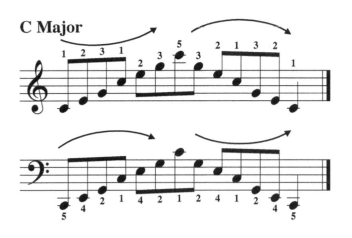

**G Major**

**D Major**

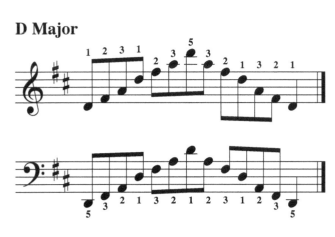

**A Major**

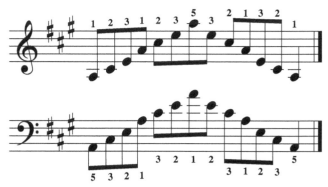

**E Major**

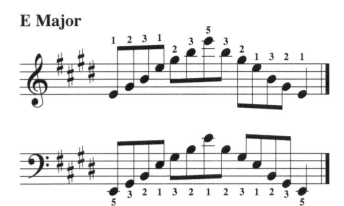

**B Major**

**F Major**

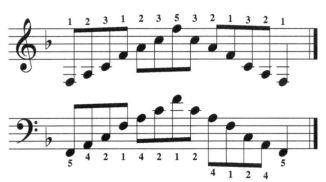

**Bb Major**

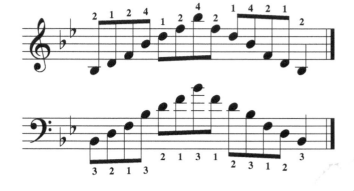

54

FF3012

**E♭ Major**

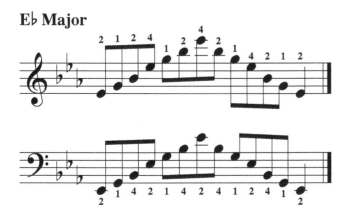

# Two-Octave Minor Arpeggios

The arrows indicate the under and over circular wrist motion for playing arpeggios.

**A minor**

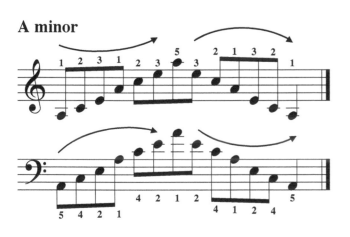

**E minor**

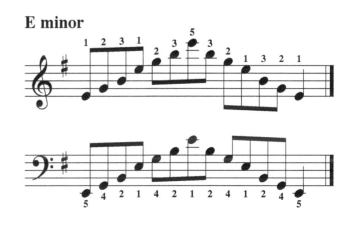

**B minor**

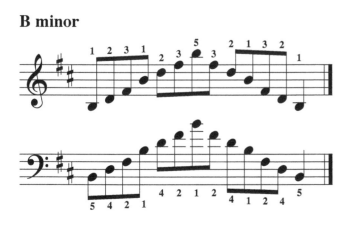

**D minor**

**G minor**

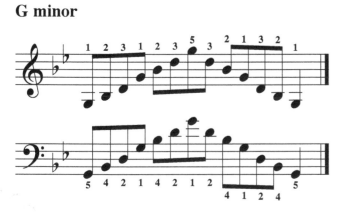

**C minor**

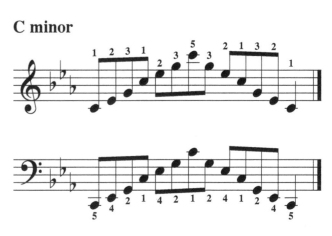

# Certificate
# of Achievement

## CONGRATULATIONS TO

_____

(Your name)

You have completed

**PIANO ADVENTURES**®

_Technique & Artistry Book_ **LEVEL 4**

Teacher: _____

Date: _____